Editor: Violeta BISCHOFF

Courseology

A proven step-by-step system to launch your online course in 3 days!

COPYRIGHT NOTICE
TABLE OF CONTENTS
PREFACE
    Get ready, steady, learn!
    How it all fits together
    Will 3 days be sufficient to launch the course?
DAY 1: PLANNING THE ADVENTURE OF THEIR LIFETIME
    Chapter 1: identify a much needed, highly sought, easily sold topic for your course
        The SDP Questionnaire
        The 4 U's Approach
        Teaching Platforms
    Chapter 2: Determine tangible outcomes for your students
        The MNS Questionnaire
    Chapter 3: Prepare an interactive curriculum that enthralls your audience
        The Curriculum Autopilot Template
        Delivery Styles
        BONUS: Test it out: get real feedback from potential students
DAY 2: CREATE HIGHLY ENGAGING CONTENT THAT MESMERIZES YOUR MARKET!
    Chapter 1: Who are you? Build an inspiring bio
        The BIOdiversity Template
    Chapter 2: Create highly engaging content that mesmerizes your market!
        The 3 Presentation Styles
        The Script Autopilot Template
        The Meta Project

Chapter 3: Convert visitors into loyal customers with a great course presentation
    The Course Presentation Template
DAY 3: PRODUCE CONTENT THAT TRANSFORMS!
    Chapter 1: Set up a cheap but effective recording studio
        Technical Equipment
        Recording Guidelines
    Chapter 2: 3, 2, 1, Action!
        Deliver Great Content
        The Dazzling Effect
    Chapter 3: Publish your magnum opus!
        The Perfect Price Challenge
OUTRO

PREFACE

Get ready, steady, learn!

 Hi, my name is Bogdan Vaida and in this book I'm going to offer you **Courseology**- a proven, step-by-step system that transforms your idea into a sellable online course in only 3 days.

This book started out as a workbook complementary to my online course with the same name, but after adding entire chapters based on the questions my students asked, it became much more.

Now, it contains the complete system used by me and many others to launch online courses in the shortest time possible while not subtracting from their quality. It is a standalone product that empowers you to build an online course from scratch, without any prior knowledge or experience.

If you are interested in the online course which features video examples, scenarios, case studies and other multimedia materials, check out the presentation page for Courseology - A proven step-by-step system to launch your online course in 3 days! at www.courseology.org .

My motto is "**I teach students how to become their own teachers!**". So this book is not about me, it's about *you* and how *you* can get the results *you* want.

Please email me at office@vaidabogdan.com for any questions, corrections, suggestions or any other kind of feedback you may have. I love interacting with my students and that would also help me keep the content up to date.

How it all fits together

While creating the book I had a very big challenge.
On one side, I had to make the process as straightforward as possible, but on the other, I also had to provide you with a great system that would double the effectiveness of each part of the process.
Therefore, I divided each section into mandatory steps and optional steps.

If you wish to create your course over the weekend, just stick to the mandatory steps, but if your goal is to launch an amazing course that will inspire your audience, then I suggest you use the whole workbook. For those of you who aim to customize, feel free to choose what best fits your personality.

My students and I have created courses over a weekend using only the mandatory steps. Examples of such courses are The Secrets of Habits and Learn Photoshop by example (available at http://courses.vaidabogdan.com). But once we had done this one or two times, we realized that we wanted to give so much more. As a result, we created a compendium of techniques (all of which comprised in this book) and thus, delivered to impress. We added templates and bonuses, Wow! effects, we upgraded our toolbox and we launched engaging courses like Test Your Personality Using The DISC Assessment Tool and Active Reviewing (available at http://courses.vaidabogdan.com). These types of courses took a bit longer to create- the maximum for me being 2 months: 1 month of co-writing the content with my editor and one month of producing and editing the videos.

However, if this is your first course, follow the mandatory steps and finish it by the end of the weekend. After that, go ahead and launch it so you can get real feedback from your audience (instead of "guessing" what else is needed). In your following courses, feel free to use the optional steps presented in the workbook to deliver a more immersive experience.

Will 3 days be sufficient to launch the course?

Let's compare the following scenarios:

Scenario 1: The Virtual Zoo idea

You love animals and you have a great idea of teaching programming online by showing students how to create a virtual Zoo. Sounds fun, right?
You set the launch date in 1 week's time, and just when you've gotten near the end (having prepared most of the videos), you realize you also need some quizzes, more reference materials and that in fact, it would be wiser to reshoot your second video. You exceed your launch date by three days. But hey, you got everything perfect.

You are very proud of your work. The group activity is about creating a virtual zoo — very creative stuff which builds upon previous knowledge in order to create a complex project. You launch and 23 days later, the statistics start rolling in.

Surprise, surprise:
- 5% of your students checked the reference materials.
- 9% did the first 3 quizzes and only 2% did the last one.
- They were all disappointed of the zoo activity. In the comments, they wrote that they would have loved a more practical project, maybe coding an iOS app .. not a zoo.

Although disappointed at first, you realize your students have provided you with a great idea. Why create a *virtual* Zoo when you can create a *real* iOS app?

So you spend an additional week creating an iOS development project from scratch and change the course title to "Become an iOS Developer from scratch" and the subtitle to "iOS 9 & Objective-C in 7 applications". Not the best title, but also not the worst. (Though you'll learn how to create a very persuasive title in the later chapters of this book).

After the relaunch, you get a boom of students and your course gets constantly recommended by bloggers and forum gurus.

Looking back, you realize that you could've saved 23 days if you'd had the courage to launch straight away, thus finding out what the paying members wanted and then dedicating those days to fulfilling their need.

Scenario 2: The good enough

Your course has average video, great audio and great content. You intend to launch, but you are a bit scared of students saying the course doesn't look professionally enough. Still, you launch.

Surprise, surprise: the feedback doesn't even mention the video. They enjoyed the course and they want templates and step-by-step procedures for your materials.

You add the requested content and suddenly, all your students say how much they appreciated that the instructor over delivered and that he added additional materials based on their needs. The course gets a lot of 5-star reviews and it becomes one of the best in its niche.

Looking back, you realize that you haven't even updated the videos because it wasn't as necessary as you thought it was. Your students had other needs.

Lessons learned

What you think your customers want and what they actually want are 2 different things that **may** or **may not** intersect.

You may think: Why don't I ask my followers what they want *before* I create the course?
Great strategy, implement it!
... as long as you don't forget that they are not actual buyers (yet). The actual buyers are only a small percentage of your followers and they probably have some very specific needs (which may be different than the needs of the larger audience answering your questions).

This is true for most markets and the business industry responded with a concrete concept that addresses the issue: the minimum viable product (**MVP**).

From Wikipedia:
"A minimum viable product has just those core features that allow the product to be deployed, and no more. The product is typically deployed to a subset of possible customers, such as early adopters that are thought to be more forgiving, more likely to give feedback, and able to grasp a product vision from an early prototype or marketing information. It is a strategy targeted at avoiding building products that customers do not want, that seeks to maximize the information learned about the customer per dollar spent. "The minimum viable product is that version of a new product which allows a team to collect the maximum amount of validated learning about customers with the least effort."

I am here to help you deliver a minimum viable course, get **feedback from the actual buyers** and then, update the content to **perfectly fit their needs**.
All of this, **without spending needless days creating content that no one cares about**.

Sounds like a plan? Well it is. And it was created based on reality, by collaborating with numerous students that wanted to launch their own course in the online environment.

DAY 1: PLANNING THE ADVENTURE OF A LIFETIME

Chapter 1: Identify a much needed, highly sought, easily sold topic for your course

Purpose: In order to deliver something that's both sellable and useful to your audience, you need an intersection of what you're good at (skill), what the market needs (demand) and what you love doing (passion). And now, I'm going to help you identify your sweet spot.

Mandatory steps: (2 hours)
1. Fill out The SDP Questionnaire to pinpoint your sweet spot.
2. Design a persuasive title by following The 4 U's Approach.
3. Read about the different Teaching Platforms available and the terminology they use.

The biggest mistake most people make at this point is taking more than 1 hour per step. At this stage you need a "good enough" course topic and a "good enough" title. Don't try to be a perfectionist; mistakes are normal, so expect them and learn from them.

Optional steps:
1. Learn a new skill:
   a. Become an expert by reading: Mastery by Robert Greene (http://amzn.to/1JZLJ0w).
   b. Use Timothy Ferriss' 4-step process for mastering any skill: The DiSSS framework (http://bit.ly/timferriss4).

The SDP Questionnaire

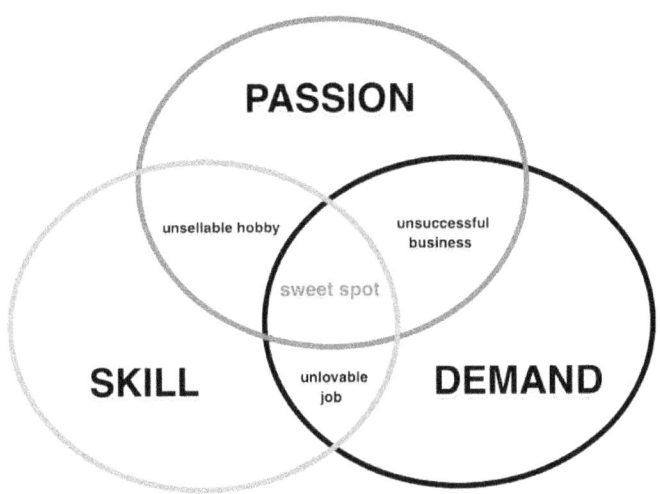

Answer the following questions to identify what you are good at (**S**kill), what the market needs (**D**emand) and what you love doing (**P**assion) — **SDP**, in order to pinpoint your sweet spot.

Identify 5-10 Skills that you are good at by answering the questions below:

- What are you naturally good at?
- What do you love doing?
- What do people ask your help for?
- What do your friends recommend you for?
- If you have a hobby, are you good at it?
- If you work, are you good at it? Do you enjoy it?
- Do you post on Facebook things you create/cook/design/program?
- What do you want to teach?
- What's your field of expertise?
- Do you have a knack for physics, public speaking or something else?

- Are you compassionate, driven or maybe a great leader?

For more help, check out these links:
  - http://jobsearch.about.com/od/list/fl/business-skills.htm
  - http://www.ceswoodstock.org/job_search/resumeskillspers.shtml
  - http://examples.yourdictionary.com/examples-of-skills.html

For more clarity, here are 3 skills we'll use as example: time management, video editing and cooking.

Check market Demand for those skills

- Who is your target audience?
  - Who are your ideal students?
  - Why are they interested in taking your course?
  - What do they want to learn?
  - What will they get out of the course?
  - What need are you solving?
  - Why should they choose your course over another similar course?
  - How does your course differ from any other similar course?
  - Does your course help with something they care about (relationships, lifestyle, career)?
- Search online course repositories like curious.com, skillshare.com and udemy.com for courses on that topic. Get your answers to the questions: How many students do they have? How much do they cost?
- Search Youtube.com for videos teaching the same topic. See if they have a huge audience That means at least 10k views and great ratings. Also, what do people in the comments ask? Do they want a different technique or a *how to* on a related topic?

- Search Quora.com for questions related to your skill. Ask yourself- would those people be interested in buying a solution?
- Search forums and blog in the industry.
- Fill the table below and rate from 1 to 5 based on how many courses in the same topic are present on those platforms. We are checking for demand; if we find a lot of courses on a particular topic, it usually means there's a high demand of that topic.

Skill	Curious	Udemy	Skillshare	Total
cooking	5 (1075 results)	0 (123 results)	1 (53 results)	6
video editing	5	4	2	11
productivity				

Find your Passion

You probably won't identify your lifelong vocation in 5 easy steps, but you can have quite a few passion projects that you are keen on doing and here we'll be figuring out which they are.

Choose from the **D**emand exercise the top 3 skills sorted by total points and from those choose one by asking you the following questions:
- If you worked only 3 days developing an online course, which of the topics would you choose?
- Are you doing something unique, interesting or novel on that topic?
  - Is your approach different?
  - Is your topic specific enough? Nobody buys "Time Management", but most managers and most people troubled by email would buy

"The Busy Manager: 21 Days to a Stress-Free Inbox."

- Can you teach it to others? Can they replicate your success? Can you show them how you work?
- Is it easy to find information on that topic on the internet? Would people pay to get a step-by-step system on that topic? Would they pay for something that gives them tangible results?
- What prices do the courses on those topics have? How many students would buy the course? What potentially financial gain would you get from launching a course in that field? Would you be able to get other benefits (authority, related part time projects, networking opportunities)?
- 3 days from today, which course would you want to have published?

My sweet spot is: …… …… …… …… …… …… …… ..

The 4 U's Approach

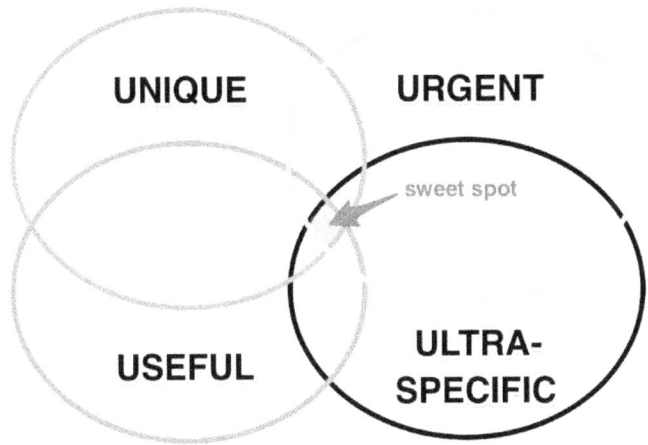

The 4 U formula states that content should be **U**seful, **U**nique, **U**ltra-specific and **U**rgent. It works wonders for course titles.

The 4 U Formula - what does each U stand for:

Useful:
- Usefulness is critical because it responds to the question: "why should I join?"
- It compels the student to keep reading.
- It provides value to your (future) students.
- Never say "learn" or "find out". Use "discover", "uncover" or "be able to" (the latter is useful in your copy, not in the title).
- E.g.: "Create your professional CV in minutes", "Discover how to draw human faces in Photoshop", "Uncover the mysteries of Photoshop: Drawing human faces".

Unique:
- "Video editing" (bad) vs. "Video editing for designers" (better) vs. "Camtasia for designers that want to get highly paid jobs" (best).

- It's critical because it helps you differentiate your course from the competitors.
  - You can differentiate by target audience (as I have done in the examples above). For whom is your course? Who is your ideal student? "Camtasia for designers"
  - By experience required: "Advanced C++ & Design Patterns"
  - Or by subtopic: "Morning habits: 10 easy hacks to keep them forever!"

Ultra-specific:
- As a student, would you buy: "Time Management" or "Time management for busy students"? As a student who always has problems organizing himself before exams would you buy "Time management for busy students" or "Study hacks: increase your marks by 2 points and still have time to play"?
- Make it as specific as possible because your audience will be more inclined to buy a course that they identify themselves with.
- Talk to your audience in their language (which you find by answering their questions and by checking forums and blogs). Does a student say "I'm busy" or "I'm studying hard"?

Urgent:
- Urgency compels the audience to buy (or continue reading/watching) in order not to miss out.
- It's the first one to be left out if you've created a great title that would lose its power by providing a sense of urgency (timeless / evergreen titles).
- E.g. "Are you losing sales by not applying these financial hacks?"

Other things to take into consideration:
- The subtitle complements the title, it doesn't rephrase it.
- If you've missed a "U" in the title, add it in the subtitle.
- The ultimate goal of (sub)titles is to connect with potential customers at an emotional level so that they will read the next piece of content.
- Fill the table below and rate from 1 to 5 how well you've used the 4 U's in your title:

Title	Useful	Unique	Ultra-specific	Urgent	Total
Video editing	3	0	0	0	3
Video editing for designers	3	2	2	0	7
Camtasia for designers that want to get a highly paid job	5	4	4	1*	14
Your Course Title					

* Urgency gets 1 here because we are hinting at getting a highly paid job which may solve other (urgent) problems.

Other tools for improving your title:
- Headline Analyzer (http://coschedule.com/headline-analyzer)
- Emotional Marketing Value Headline Analyzer (http://www.aminstitute.com/headline/)

Take the results of these analyzers with a grain of salt as they will never "get" a title like humans do.

My course title is: ……………………………………..

Teaching Platforms

When publishing an online course, check the Terms of Service of the platform where you are going to publish your course. On the majority of the platforms, you have full rights to the content, including redistributing the course materials.

What this means is that you can publish your course on multiple platforms.

In this document, I'm going to provide you with a list of the best online course marketplaces that I personally use and their curse taxonomy:

1. **www.udemy.com**

"academy of you"

Help link: https://teach.udemy.com/process/

- Course
  - Sections
    - Lectures (5'-7' videos)
      - Resources
        - Files (attachments)
        - External resources (URL)
        - Source code
      - Captions
      - Q&A section
    - Quizzes
      - Multiple choice

- Coding exercises (HTML, CSS, Javascript, Java)

Exporting:
https://support.udemy.com/customer/portal/articles/1980990-video-quality-optimal-video-export-settings
Recording:
https://support.udemy.com/customer/portal/articles/1980918
Video Quality Standards:
https://support.udemy.com/customer/portal/articles/1717206-recording-video-right-the-first-time-quality-standards?b_id=3056

2. www.curious.com

Help link: https://curious.com/teach/learning-center

- Course
  - Course overview video
  - Lessons (2'-30')
    - Sections (1-3')
      - Exercises
        - True/false
        - Multiple choice
    - Attachments
      - Photos
      - Files
      - External links
      - Amazon links
    - Discussions

3. www.skillshare.com

A platform to learn anything, from anyone.

Help link: https://www.skillshare.com/teach/handbook

- Class
    - Video lessons (10'-25')
    - Community
    - Class Project
        - Attachments
    - Project Gallery

Exporting: http://help.skillshare.com/hc/en-us/articles/204543358-Technical-Specifications-Exporting-and-Uploading-
Class publishing checklist:
https://www.skillshare.com/teach/handbook/review-class-checklist/205222657

4. www.avanoo.com

AVANOO

Avanoo has a different approach to online learning. It delivers daily 3' videos on various topics.

The process is also distinct:
1. You receive Word templates for the course curriculum, for the daily 3' video and for your bio.
2. You fill the templates with your content.
3. Once they approve, you narrate the text.
4. They add the video to the text (usually an inspiring or relaxing video).

5. www.teachable.com

It's not a course marketplace, but it allows you to host your courses on your own domain.

- Course
  - Sections
    - Lectures
      - Text
      - Quizzes
        - True/False
        - Multiple Choice
      - Comments
      - Attachments
      - Captions

6. Text / email lessons

Old-school, I know.
Still, email lessons have some specific benefits:
- Many readers love them.
- The material can be read from an eBook reader.
- Content can be quickly copied somewhere (e.g. Lines of code).
- If your reader knows 80% of the content, they can skim until they find something new.

Media can also be added to email lessons: PDFs, images, graphics.

If there's one idea I'd want to leave you with, then it's this: create a course and publish it on all of these platforms!

Chapter 2: Determine tangible outcomes for your students

Purpose: People don't buy information, they buy solutions. Offer a **M**uch **N**eeded **S**olution for a need they have and they will buy your course.

Mandatory steps: (30 minutes)
1. Fill The MNS Questionnaire to find out what your students actually need.

The biggest mistake most people make at this point is not thinking in terms of what a real prospect. Ask yourself: would you buy this solution if another trainer would provide this course? What would they need to give you in order for you to take the money out of your pockets?

Optional steps:
1. Create a Fakebook (http://www.classtools.net/FB/home-page) profile of your ideal customer, keep it updated and speak in his/her language.
2. Create an empathy map (https://vimeo.com/27832845).
3. Read Ask: The Counterintuitive Online Formula to Discover Exactly What Your Customers Want to Buy...Create a Mass of Raving Fans...and Take Any Business to the Next Level (http://amzn.to/1LrtsVb). Why? Well .. read the title again.
4. Here's a sample ideal customer: http://bit.ly/avatar-lee-loffler .

The MNS Questionnaire

Answer the following questions to identify your students' **M**uch **N**eeded **S**olution. While you answer them, keep in mind what you identified in the previous chapter (your sweet spot and your course title).

Identify your target audience:
- What's inside your prospect's mind?
    a. What are their beliefs (opinion, attitude, prejudice)?
    b. What do they desire (physical, material, sensual)?
    c. What do they identify with (traits, roles in life)?
- What's their biggest pain point?
- Who should take this course?
- Who shouldn't take this course? If your course is for beginners, don't sell it as being for everyone or you'll

get a lot of unsatisfied customers that know the topic and were seeking an advanced course.
- Where do they spend their time? (Facebook, Twitter, blogs, newspapers, offline conventions, with their family)

Provide tangible results:
- What tangible results will my students have? Phrase the answer in terms of what they get out of it, instead of what information they learn.
- What new skills will they use once they finish the course? The skills they get need to be specific and new or at least greatly improved.
- Will their lives be transformed by having these results that you're promising? How?
- How will your course solve their problem?
- Why do they need those results?
- When will they get the results? What prevents them from getting those results sooner? (You set their expectations and you tell them what (and when) the course will actually be delivered. This is also great for reviews because they can check to see if you've fulfilled your promise.)
- Do they need qualifications or specific skills before enrolling? Do they need to take a specific action or a previous course? Or maybe a personality test to identify how they learn best.

Course feature	What's in it for them?
Step-by-step templates	You follow the course on auto-pilot. You never get lost. You always know the next step. You won't fall prey to the common mistakes. You will do minimal work. No stress involved.
A new system	You will be a leader in the field and gain followers, partners and an entire community ready to join your work.

Discover the Much Needed Solution

Fill in:

At the end of the course, you will be able to _____ which means that you will _____ which also means that _____ .

Here's an example for a course titled **"Camtasia for designers that want to get highly paid jobs"**:
At the end of my course, you will be able to **create amazing videos** which means that you will **mesmerize your viewers instantly** which also means that you **get a highly paid job in no time**.
And that actually gave me an idea for a headline: **"Create amazing videos that mesmerize your viewers instantly!"**

And now, a final story!

Kevin Rogers, founder of Copy Chief (http://copychief.com/), explained in his private mastermind group how to identify the emotional avatar of your customer, how to find out why they really buy your product and how to identify the deep emotion under the logical reason.

My friend and mentor, John Carlton, has a great saying that every customer, every prospect, everyone who's ever bought anything... has the reason they SAY they buy, and the reason they REALLY buy.

So, on this line:

His main ambition is to look and feel fit and healthy so he can be a role model for his children and so that he can rekindle the passion he and his wife once experienced.

... I'm going to call bullsh*t.

Nobody wakes up from a deep sleep, panting with anxiety and says: "I need to look and feel fit so I can be a better role model!"

Why?

It's too practical. We need to drill down into this man's psyche and discover what's really eating at him. Somebody made a comment that, although he brushed it off with a chuckle, stuck him deep.

"Damn Jim... what bra size are you up to these days?"

Or maybe there was an incident with his kids that served as the turning point.

His daughter begged him to go down the waterslide with her. He was reluctant because he's big and doesn't like climbing stairs, but that little voice popped up and said, "you know, she's 10 now... in two more years she won't be asking anymore."

So he gave in, and even though the journey up those stairs was brutal, he embraced the moment. Joking with his daughter, talking about how fun the slide will be. It felt good to be "plugged in". These are the small moments that make up a life.

Then, as they approached the top, he saw the sign and his heart sunk: Weight Limit 275 pounds. He knew he was probably over that, but hopefully didn't look it. Maybe he'll slide by.

"Sir, can I ask you to hop on the scale for me real quick?" The fit young attendant said to him. "It's an insurance thing. If anyone overcapacity goes down and slams the wall we get in big trouble."

Now, the whole line, it seemed, was listening and watching. Annoyed at the fat dude holding up the ride. Not wanting to make more of a scene, he stepped on the scale. Sure enough, he was "over capacity". A whole ten pounds over.

Damn.

How did this happen?

His own denial slapped him across the face. Stinging more than slamming the wall would of, he was sure.

"It's fine dad. I'll go alone." His daughter said. Clearly embarrassed for him but wanting to reduce the sting.

His heart sunk. "Okay, sweetie. I'll meet you at the bottom."

The worst part was still in front of him.

Squeezing his way down all those stairs, past the more qualified riders.

His decided right then... ENOUGH. I've got to do something about this.

Take your time with the avatar. Think it through. Where does it hurt? What nightmare gets your prospect pacing the floor at night?

Terms like "role model" are ideas. However, it's the emotions we need to understand before our prospects will believe we truly understand, and can help.

Chapter 3: Prepare an interactive curriculum that enthralls your audience

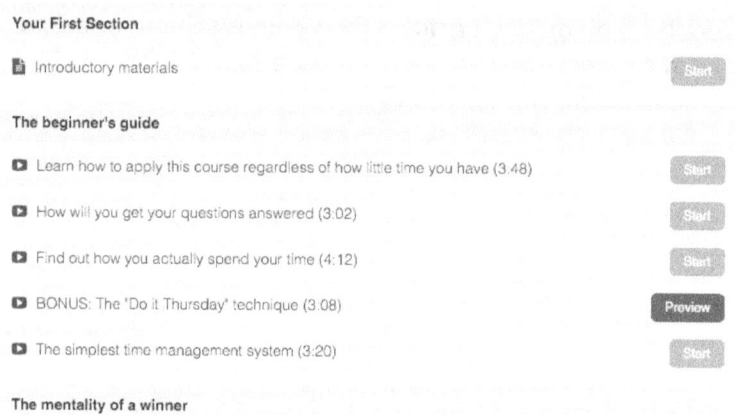

Your First Section

📄 Introductory materials — Start

The beginner's guide

▶ Learn how to apply this course regardless of how little time you have (3.48) — Start

▶ How will you get your questions answered (3:02) — Start

▶ Find out how you actually spend your time (4:12) — Start

▶ BONUS: The 'Do it Thursday' technique (3.08) — Preview

▶ The simplest time management system (3:20) — Start

The mentality of a winner

Purpose: Prospects check the curriculum to see how comprehensive it is or if it touches the subject they are most interested in. After you convert them to students, the curriculum helps them see where the course starts, what lesson they will be studying and when the course will end. It gives them direction and motivation to pursue the course until the end and it also increases retention and enables easy content consumption.

Let's look at the following example: Andrew is a busy manager who is constantly interrupted by his team. He is desperately looking for a time management course.
He sees my course on The Secrets of Time (http://courses.vaidabogdan.com) and notices that I have an entire section dedicated to managing interruptions.
It hits his pain point so he instantly buys it and jumps straight to section 5. He devours that content, applies the techniques, gets results and then relaxes and enjoys the rest of the course.
Andrew is a happy customer!
Mandatory steps: (1 hour)

1. Generate your curriculum on autopilot using The Curriculum Autopilot Template
2. Identify what kind of lectures you will use in your course by selecting from the Delivery Styles. I recommend that you use talking head for your first and last video, to show some of your personality.

The biggest mistake most people make at this point is thinking too much. Fill in the curriculum template, choose 2 or 3 delivery styles and jump to the next lesson. If you don't have a video camera, not even a smartphone, use PowerPoint or Keynote and a microphone. No big deal. It's your first course and your audience will tell you if this is enough. Don't think ahead, let reality show you the way because you don't yet have the experience to presume correctly.

Optional steps:
1. Mixing different delivery styles helps maintain the student's attention.
2. Add interviews with people that are perceived as an authority in the field.
3. Add interviews with people that have big audiences (bloggers, podcasters). Get interviewed by them or interview them by asking their opinion on the subject (e.g. If it's a time management course, ask them how do they manage their time or how do they react to missed deadlines). They'll love sharing the interview with their audience which will get you students and fans.

The Curriculum Autopilot Template

A well-structured curriculum helps students see the big picture, where they will start and what they will create. Use this template to create your curriculum by filling it in. It's fast and easy-breezy :)

Recommendations

First, make sure you abide by the conditions specific to the platform you'll use to post your course. Here are my recommendations:

Lessons:
- First lesson presents the course curriculum and tells students what they will get if they follow through.
- Prove to them that the course delivers, right from the start! Ideally, give them something to create from the first lesson so that they know it is real. This also motivates them to continue with the lessons. For example, in a course about video editing using Camtasia, I teach them from the very first lesson how to quickly edit an iPhone video in order to publish it on Facebook.
- Last lesson provides next steps and ways for them to contact you.
- Each lesson teaches one and only one concept. You can verify this by taking out a video from the course (imagine publishing it on YouTube). Does it teach one and only one clear concept?
- Each "chapter" should encompass all the lessons that teach a very specific topic. After the students finish a chapter, they should be able to do something tangible with the information that they have. Ideally, the last lesson is an activity that shows them how to do exactly that.

- Think: <u>one tangible result per chapter</u> (or one strong takeaway).
- Teach simple stuff at the beginning and expert stuff at the end.
- Add a lesson about common mistakes and another one about best practices.
- Keep everything modular.

Activities:
- Each chapter should have an activity or an exercise.
- Create activities that provide tangible results. Don't create activities to explain concepts; teach concepts that generate activities. For example, don't create an imaginary airport when you teach iOS programming, create a game that they can actually play.
- Quizzes are good when students need to remember things. They are useless when students can simply search for that information (think of when you were forced to remember things in high school).
- You can add a worksheet that they need to fill which contains:
  - Reflection questions.
  - A cheat sheet that will help them better remember the material.
  - Key takeaways.
- Add a physical activity or a mental puzzle. (E.g. For a math course, give them a problem that needs a creative answer; for a programming course, give them a piece of code that they need to debug.)
- Invite students to answer a question or solve a puzzle. Make it real (e.g. for a history course, ask them what would have happened with X peace treaty if the battle had been lost). This generates interaction and also shows that the course is a lively one.

Here's the curriculum of my Secrets of Time
(http://courses.vaidabogdan.com) course:

Chapter	Lesson	Expected outcome	Practical exercise or unique feature	Description
1		Getting the first proof that the course works.		The Beginner's Guide.
1	1	Understanding the process and having a wide view of the course.	Download the accompanying guide.	Introduce the course, why it is useful and what students will get at the end. Provide a zoom out of the whole process.
	2	Motivation to watch the rest of the materials.	The 5x5x5 Method.	Learn how to apply this course no matter how little time you have.
	3	Motivation to ask questions inside the membership site.	Ways to contact me.	How will you get your questions answered.
	4	Detecting where they spend their time by using an app or pen & paper.	Rescue Time and 2 other tricks.	Find out how you actually spend your time.
	5	Getting results from the first few materials.	My unique, highest rated technique to double the	BONUS: The "Do It Thursday" Technique.

			amount of free time.	
	6	Getting results from the first few materials.	A system they can use that very day.	The simplest time management system.
2		Developing a strong mentality in order to improve their productivity habits.		The mentality of a winner.
2	1	Ability to differentiate between how the losers think and how the winners think.		The failure / success mentality.
..	..	..	..	...
6	1	Knowing what to do next.		Closing words and next steps.

Ok ok, so how does it look in real life?
Well... like this:

Class Curriculum

Your First Section

📄 Introductory materials   [Start]

The beginner's guide

▶ Learn how to apply this course regardless of how little time you have (3:48)   [Start]

▶ How will you get your questions answered (3:02)   [Start]

▶ Find out how you actually spend your time (4:12)   [Start]

▶ BONUS: The "Do It Thursday" technique (3:06)   [Preview]

▶ The simplest time management system (3:20)   [Start]

The mentality of a winner

▶ The failure / success mentality (1:44)   [Start]

📄 BONUS SPEECH: I AM A CHAMPION   [Start]

📄 YOUTUBE: THE SECRET POWERS OF TIME   [Start]

▶ How do you perceive the passage of time (3:48)   [Start]

▶ The simplest way to transform "wasted time" into "saved time" (3:01)   [Start]

▶ My secret habit (3:37)   [Start]

▶ Why I NEVER have regrets (+exercise) (4:58)   [Start]

Fight against procrastination

▶ Eliminate decision-making: only make the first step! (1:45)   [Start]

▶ The real way to get rid of your dependencies (experiment) (3:48)   [Start]

📄 SURVEY: Training progress   [Start]

▶ The "do tomorrow what can be done today" system – improved (3:23)   [Start]

▶ Now you're at a critical point! (3:23)   [Start]

How to focus on your priorities regardless of interruptions

▶ The importance of doable tasks (7:20)   [Preview]

▶ Only work on tasks that you can finish now (2:47)   [Start]

▶ Stress: solutions and resolutions (6:24)   [Start]

📄 BONUS EXERCISE: HOW TO RELIEVE STRESS   [Start]

▶ What to do if you have a tendency to keep postponing things (2:07)   [Start]

▶ You can't keep up with the materials? (2:08)   [Start]

Vision – plan your objectives so that you can easily fulfill them

▶ The "try everything, stick only to what has results" mentality (2:05)   [Start]

▶ Assigning tasks: anyone can have an assistant (4:51)   [Start]

📄 BONUS: HOW VISUAL GOAL SETTING WILL CHANGE YOUR LIFE   [Start]

▶ How to keep your personal and professional lives balanced (1:57)   [Start]

📄 7 simple ways to say no   [Start]

📄 BONUS: Your Core Values Test (or how to do the right choice)   [Start]

▶ BONUS: The Pyramid Technique (4:26)   [Start]

Outro

▶ Closing words (1:08)   [Start]

Now you're probably thinking "I've got you! There's no way you developed that course in only 3 days!". And you are both right and wrong.

The course was launched in 3 days, but it contained only **The Beginner's Guide** (which was the whole course at that time). It delivered value and the participants asked for something more, but very specific at the same time : "how to focus and how to fight procrastination"- their words.

That's when chapters 3 and 4 appeared. And little by little, I built everything into a very comprehensive course. Nevertheless, the course was launched quickly, which enabled me to find out exactly what my students wanted and deliver the next videos tailored to their particular needs.

Now it's your turn!

Fill in the table below and show me your work!

Chapter	Lesson	Expected outcome	Exercise or unique feature	Description

Delivery Styles

1. Talking head (https://youtu.be/s3u_FRz-4RA) is great for engaging all the senses and maintaining the students' interest. I definitely recommend it:
   - For your first video, in order to show some personality, establish rapport and build trust.
   - For your last video, where you tell the students what the next steps are.
   - For your promo video, in which you present the course.
   - And it's also great for non-technical courses, where body language is expressive enough to convey the message.

2.   Screen recording (https://youtu.be/QYankg9Mug0) is great for technical courses (when editing audios, videos or photos or when programming).

3.   Audio lectures (https://app.avanoo.com/my/author?id=6631) are good for meditations, thinking, brainstorming and situations where they need to close their eyes and use their imagination

4.   Presentations (PowerPoint, Keynote, Prezi or others — https://youtu.be/m87qIC_LRno?t=20s) are perfect for showing complex visuals or when listing things (like bullet lists). You can also narrate them as an alternative to the talking head style.

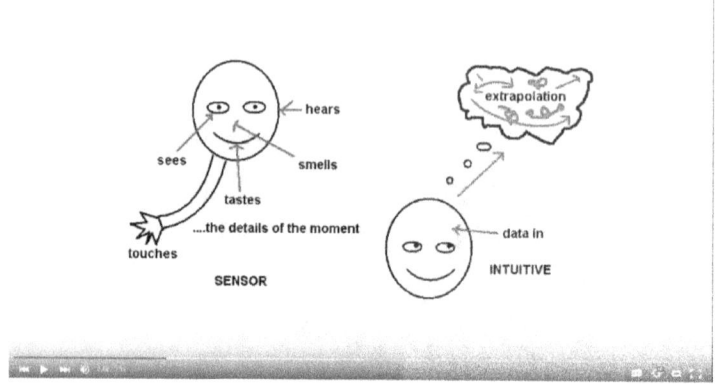

5. <u>Animations</u> (https://youtu.be/UV_ONhDss3w) are great for role plays and showing scenarios.

6. <u>Interviews</u> (https://youtu.be/A1lj8VsR4e0) give your students the opportunity to get another point of view and learn from a person who has a different approach to the matter (or a complementary view). Interviewing an authority on the subject (or a V.I.P. in the field) is also a way to boost up on trust.

7.   Documents (including online ones like http://freemultimediaguide.vaidabogdan.com) are perfect for checklists, templates and handouts. Your students can also print them and do offline assignments.

		Details	Notes
1			
2	http://pixabay.com/		great resource, royalty free, no attribution
3	http://www.freeimages.com/	no attrib req	great resource, --
4	http://commons.wikimedia.org/wiki/Main_Page		--
5	http://www.everystockphoto.com/		---
6	http://search.creativecommons.org		--
7	http://www.photoree.com		-
8	http://www.vecteezy.com/	free vector art	can be used to create images in Sparkol
9	https://unsplash.com/	photo backgroun	10 creative commons images in 10 days
10	http://photodune.net/	1$+	
11	graphicriver.net	1$+	
12	http://www.istockphoto.com/		+
13	http://deviantart.com		-- check photo ownership
14			
15	INFOGRAPHICS		
16			
17	https://infogr.am/		untested
18			

I will deliver in the following styles: (3 max)

- ………………………………………
- ………………………………………
- ………………………………………

BONUS: Test it out: get real feedback from potential students

Purpose: Before recording the content you should test how your future students will react to it. In this chapter we will gather that feedback in order to launch a course that fits your audience's needs.

Mandatory steps: (1 hour)
1. Contact 10 followers in real time (check if they are online on Skype/Facebook) and give them the written copy. Don't use email, it will take too much time and your mail may get ignored and your reply postponed.
2. Frame it as an insider's view on the upcoming content and ask for a quick feedback (2-3' of their time).
3. Ask:

a. How would you rate this course? On a scale from 1 to 10? It's better than asking them if they'd buy it. They may feel like you're trying to sell, not gather intel.

b. Does it sound like you would get something practical at the end?

c. What lessons are you interested in? What content would you skip if you wouldn't have enough time?

d.   When would you know that this course was a good investment? At the end of the course or after you would have done the project? Maybe later? How would you measure that?

e.   What's the one thing you could do to improve the course tenfold?

    4. 30' later, you have all the feedback you needed, so you can work on improving the curriculum.

The biggest mistake most people make at this point is to ask feedback from friends. Even if they have the time to help, they are not in the shoes of a potential buyer. So their feedback will be guesswork and it won't help that much. If you really don't know anybody who would be interested in purchasing your course, join social media and convince a person to check out the content (while also developing those rusty sales skills).

Optional steps:
- You can pre-sell your course to those followers. Give them a huge discount because it's a pre-pre launch and promise to create the course based on their feedback. Basically you are creating the course with them.
- You can create a survey using Google Forms (https://www.google.com/forms/about/) where you show your curriculum and ask those questions. The next step is to email the survey to your list or post it in places where your potential buyers spend their time looking (forums, blogs).

DAY 2: CREATE HIGHLY ENGAGING CONTENT THAT MESMERIZES YOUR MARKET!

Chapter 1: Who are you? Build an inspiring bio!

Purpose: Students want the best teachers they can get. They are curious and want to know who their instructor is, what she does and especially how she can help. They also need to establish connection and trust with their trainer, we are going to take care of these needs.

I injected this chapter here so that you can get some writing experience before going straight for the content.

Mandatory steps: (40 minutes)
1. Complete The BIOdiversity Template.
2. Notice how I show personality in the template and ask yourself: "How can I do something similar in my course content?"
3. Jump to the next lesson :)

The biggest mistake most people make at this point is either not having a bio (thus losing a great opportunity to show authority and to create some trust) or having a bloated bio (which is unreadable to busy prospects).

Optional steps:
- Just like before, you can ask the same people for feedback on your bio.
- Check curious.com, skillshare.com or udemy.com for top courses in your field. Which course would you buy based only on the instructor's bio?

The BIOdiversity Template

Who is Bogdan Vaida

Bogdan Vaida burst onto the training scene in 2009 using extremely old Powerpoint presentations. Luckily, 2 years later he switched to experiential trainings and learning by doing, methodologies that he practiced devotedly into all of his trainings. Known for his no-nonsense approach to getting results, Bogdan has been told that he helps participants get their own "insanely practical insights".

What does he do? He travels around the world doing experiential trainings in fields ranging from time management to personality typologies and trainer training.
While doing this he also manages his online courses that have over 7624 students from all over the world.

In 2015 he beat the record for total time spent in airports.

If you want to see what he is teaching just do one of the tests on the Online Personality Tests page.

Recommendations:
- Use a professional image.
- Keep your bio short and concise.
- Make it relevant to your topic.
- Don't just say that you are an expert, show the reason why you are that expert.
- Show authority / credibility / social proof:
    - Quotes from students.
    - Numbers (# of courses, # of students, # of positive ratings).
    - Companies you've worked with.
- Throw in your motto, a favorite inspiring song, your very own catchphrase, the name of your pet... you get it!
- Write it in the 3rd person. Why? It sounds better, it promotes objectivity and you don't appear like you are your own desperate publicity agency.

Here's a sample :)

Let's anatomize my bio from www.vaidabogdan.com:
(Quick definition: besides dissecting a body, anatomize also means
analyzing in detail.)
Very quick tip: In your course, you can show personality using
"combos" like what I did above when I've used a secondary,
obscure meaning of a common word. This way, you are also
teaching something interesting other than your field, in short bursts!

Bogdan Vaida burst onto the training scene in 2009 using extremely old
PowerPoint presentations. Luckily, 2 years later he switched to
experiential trainings and learning by doing, methodologies that he
practiced devotedly into all of his trainings. Known for his no-nonsense
approach to getting results, Bogdan has been told that he helps
participants get their own "insanely practical insights".

What does he do? He travels around the world doing experiential
trainings in fields ranging from time management to personality
typologies and trainer training.
While doing this, he also manages his online courses that have over 7624
students from all over the world.

In 2015 he beat the record for total time spent in airports.

If you want to see what he is teaching just do one of the tests on the
Online Personality Tests page

And here's the same discourse, broken down into parts:

Bogdan Vaida burst onto the training scene in 2009 using
extremely old PowerPoint presentations. *("Who is he?" Students
need to feel close to me so I've introduced myself in a funny way.)*
Luckily, 2 years later he switched to experiential trainings and
learning by doing, methodologies that he practiced devotedly
into all of his trainings. Known for his no-nonsense approach to
getting results, Bogdan has been told that he helps participants
get their own "insanely practical insights". *("How can the trainer
help me?" Here I show the "how" part of my method. I also hint at
the online courses as a second way of helping my students.)*

What does he do? He travels around the world doing experiential trainings in fields ranging from time management to personality typologies and trainer training.

While doing this, he also manages his online courses that have over 7624 students from all over the world. *("Is he competent to teach? Does he help a lot of people?" This is the social proof / authority part.)*

In 2015 he beat the record for total time spent in airports. *("Is he likeable?" I add a funny experience to show some personality.)*

If you want to see what he is teaching just do one of the tests on the Online Personality Tests page. *("Is he accessible?" I'm inviting them to connect in the email with the test results.)*

Another quick tip: this is a visual method for highlighting "stuff" like changes, corrections and comments. I invite you to use it in your courses!

Now it's your turn!

Let's see the skeleton of a great looking bio:
(Notice how I make a reference to the dissection joke. You can personalize an entire lecture based on a pun, thus keeping your discourse light and funny and your students attentive.)

1. Introduce yourself

Question that needs to be answered: What's this page about? Who is he / she (the trainer)?

Start with your name, the reader needs to realize what they are reading (especially if it's an external page to which they may get on through some other medium).

Tell them how you started. It helps create a feeling of closeness (he / she was in my shoes once). Remember! Familiarity breeds sales!
You can start with "Not so long ago I was.."

```
┌─────────────────────────────────────────────────┐
│                                                   │
│                                                   │
│                                                   │
│                                                   │
│                                                   │
└─────────────────────────────────────────────────┘
```

2. Display your claim of fame

Question that needs to be answered: How can he/she help me?

It needs to be related to the topic at hand. Also show some accomplishments.
Basically here you hook the reader and entice him / her to continue reading.
Think: "with my technique, which increased sales by 300% during my year at the company…"

```
┌─────────────────────────────────────────────────┐
│                                                   │
│                                                   │
│                                                   │
│                                                   │
│                                                   │
└─────────────────────────────────────────────────┘
```

3. Provide social proof

Questions that need to be answered: Is the trainer competent to teach me? Did his/her students achieve success? Did he/she help others like me? Why should I trust him/her?

Here you need to show some social proof to demonstrate that you are an authority in the field, that you are credible. You can also add a quote from one of your students.

Think: "my book Personality Boost was on Amazon's Best Seller's list for 2 consecutive months", "I helped 3 Fortune 500 CEOs achieve an increase in profits of", "...over 2000 students".

4. Show some personality

Question that needs to be answered: Do I like him/her?

You can write a short bio and ask a mastermind/copywriting group for suggestions on how to inject some personality or learn to do it yourself, by example. You have models all over this template and also below:

Not so good: "Bogdan Vaida spoke in public for X years"
Way better: "Bogdan Vaida burst onto the training scene"

Not so good: "Einstein invented the theory of relativity. He was born.."
Way better: "Einstein invented TIME! And now it's time to figure out how.." (<-- Ok, maybe not my best joke. Can you "upgrade" Einstein's bio?)

Not so good: "Dracula was the prince of Wallachia. He reigned during 1448, 1456–1462 and 1476."
Way better: "He got rid of all the sick and poor — by burning them alive. Nicknamed The Prince of Terror, he ruled Wallachia 3 times, between 1448 and 1476."

Notice how I also gave an out-of-context example, maybe even 2. Having 2 serious examples and a funny one helps keep things light, maintain attention and it also shows some personality. Oh, and I really hope you like my jokes. No hate mail please!)

5. Invite personal contact

Questions that need to be answered: Is he/she accessible? Can I ask the trainer something (maybe about buying one of the courses)?

Having a way for readers to contact you is optional but useful. Even if you don't have one in your bio, have one a link away from the bio (a "Contact" page maybe).

Sometimes potential buyers read your bio and they want to contact you either for work for hire or to ask something about one of your courses that they intend to buy.
My bio shows that I'm available to hold trainings in other countries; a simple sentence which generated quite a few opportunities.

P.S. Notice how in the previous page, I gave you tables that you needed to fill. Here, on the other hand, you have empty boxes for writing and, at the end, you combine everything into your bio. Use any of these methods in your courses, but don't combine them. Maintain the format through the course.

P.P.S. I'm combining them to show you different ways of doing things so don't criticize and... enjoy! :)

Chapter 2: Create highly engaging content that mesmerizes your market!

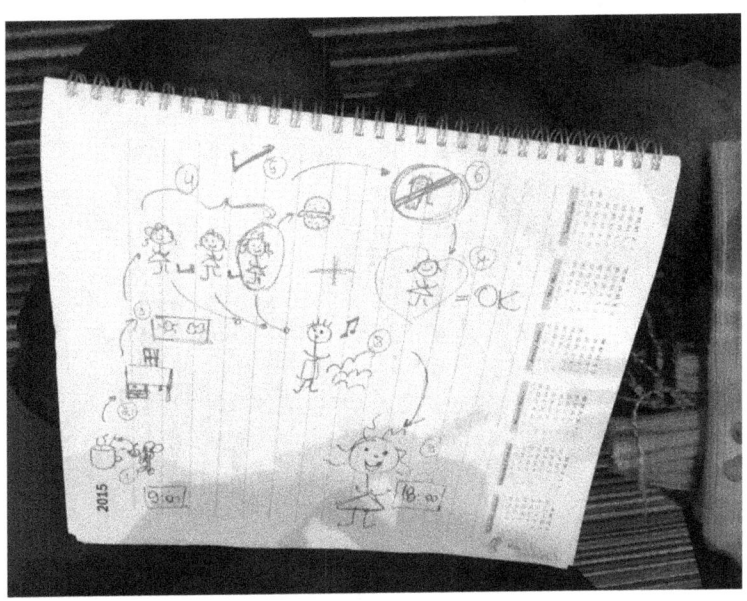

Purpose: Time to write — not too much though (remember, it's **3 Days to your Online Course**). Depending on your personality, you actually have 3 ways of doing things: presenting on the spot (for the creative talkers out there) and reading from a prompter (for the pure perfectionists). Wondering what's the third one? Don't stop reading...

Mandatory steps: (4 hours)
1. Find out your style by reading The 3 Presentation Styles.
2. Write your masterpiece on autopilot using The Script Autopilot Template.
3. Develop The Meta Project that empowers your students to replicate your success.

The biggest mistake most people make at this point is trying to write the perfect script. Perfectionists beware! If you postpone releasing the content, what actually happens is that you write a script that's perfect for you but not necessarily for your audience. What you need to do instead is to release as quickly as possible, get feedback regarding your audience's exact needs and then, write to perfection. Here you go; you now have a moment in time where you can use your perfectionism. Enjoy!)

Optional steps:
- Join the National Novel Writing Month (http://nanowrimo.org/) project to speed up your writing process.
- You can use online brainstorming (https://bubbl.us/) tools to generate ideas for course content, exercises, stories, examples, lesson names, etc.

The 3 Presentation Styles

1. The scriptwriter
- Great for perfectionists.
- And a must for non-native speakers as they can concentrate on delivering with a proper accent and on spelling the words correctly instead of dividing their attention and trying to be creative.
- Delivery is accurate, well-thought-out.
- It's difficult to emote while talking to a wall.
- It can sound robotic at times, without the "proverbial "spark.
- Writing the content takes quite some time.
- But the script can be quickly repurposed into a book.

2. The talker:

- Great for extroverts and people who love talking.
- It shows how passionate you are; your content flows naturally.
- You sometimes wander off and even forget content.
- It's pretty darn hard to be concise when you're not following a script.

- Producing the content takes more time (multiple takes, lots of editing).
- Usually the content is longer which makes the course appear 'heavier'.
- But your mistakes are easily accepted by the public because they see how natural you are.

"Antrenament" pentru a vorbi cu succes în public

3. The middleman

- Great if you are neither interested in writing the whole content down, nor in doing the delivery on the spot.
- Works well with short lessons (1-3') because you don't have time to go down the rabbit hole.
- You usually need to get a few takes (fewer than if you talked on the spot and definitely more than if you have the content pre-written).

(I'm the scriptwriter type and one of the advantages of writing all that content down is that you can quickly publish it into a book.)

After reading the descriptions of the three types, I conclude I am the …………………………………………..

The Script Autopilot Template

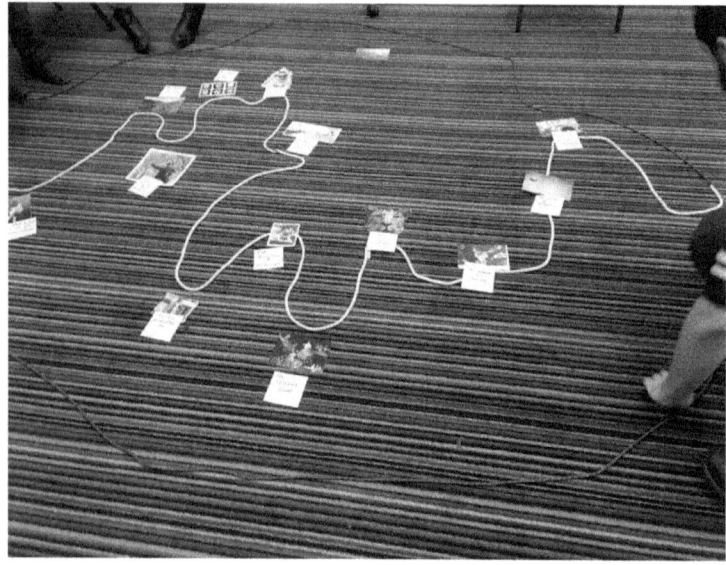

This template can be used to create content for each lecture in the course. It is based on the 3 presentation styles described previously. It can go very shallow, giving you some pointers when you deliver, or extremely deep, generating the full content that you can later repurpose as a book.

As a reminder, the 3 levels are:
1. Talker: just some main points that you can skim over before talking on camera.
2. Middleman: an outline of what you're going to talk about, metaphors you're going to use, names of stories you're going to tell.
3. Scriptwriter: you write everything, A to Z, including the jokes you're going to say on camera.

Note that what follows is only a template. If you have other ideas on how to write the content, I am always excited to hear and learn something new! Contact me and tell me more about it :)

Below you have some recommendations:

- Use "you" instead of "we". Refer directly to your student, don't generalize. (E.g. Rephrase "And this can help **us** deliver" to "And this can help **you** deliver").
- Explain potential misunderstandings your students may have. It shows that you know with what situations they may struggle.
- Also explain the jargon/terminology that you're going to use.
- Write around 200-500 words per concept - that's around 2-5 minutes of speech. If your concept is more complex than that, split it into sub concepts that can be delivered 3' at a time. It helps maintain the attention and retention of the audience.

Here's a sample :)

I've created the script for the lesson on the spot by responding to the questions from the first column. It's not my best and not my worst, but if you put 2 and 2 together, the content of this lesson is a viable time management technique that works in real life.

Introduction	Talker	Middleman	Scriptwriter
Why should they listen?	the why	about: how to free time when busy	In this lesson you will learn how to free time to do the important stuff in your day no matter how busy you are.
What are you going to talk about?	DIT	Do It Thursday: counterintuitive + wonders busy schedule	The Do It Thursday technique is counterintuitive but it can work wonders in

			your busy schedule.
In which situation can they put the information into practice?	++tasks	a lot of tasks, postponing them	If you have a lot of tasks and you keep postponing the important things that you know you need to do, read on.

Body	Talker	Middleman	Scriptwriter
Story that illustrates main point, agitates the problem and may or may not deliver the solution	DIT story	DIT story: 7 years, 3 jobs (lying 2 jobs), sports, dancing. Full To-do, unimportant tasks. Busy Sunday, postponing to Thursday => free up Sunday. Worked at dissertation + project.	I figured out this technique 7 years ago when I was at university and I've been using it ever since. Back then, I had 3 jobs (though in my time management trainings I've always told people I had 2 jobs; 3 is way too unbelievable). I was also doing sports, going out every weekend and learning how to dance. My TODO list was full of stuff and I always prioritized doing the unimportant things and postponing the real work. Then, one Sunday, I took all the things I had jotted down on my TODO and I postponed everything until the next Thursday. My day was suddenly free and I dedicated it to writing my dissertation and finishing another project that I had stalled for a very long time. It was the most productive Sunday ever and, on realizing the power of the technique, I kept using it over and over again.
Main point	how	Move all tasks	So here's how you can apply

	to DIT	to last Thursday; move to this Thursday; leave extremely urgent. 57 tasks -> 3 tasks Add important project.	this technique in your busy schedule: Take all the tasks that you have to do today and move them to the last Thursday of the month. If there are some tasks that are urgent and that you are sure would have a very bad repercussion if postponed, move them to this Thursday. And if there are some extremely urgent tasks that you need to do today, leave them be. Suddenly, out of 57 tasks you have today, you are left with 3 or 4. Then, add the most important project that you were postponing this whole week and start working on it. You have the time now, because your day is free.
Example of applying main point			(I'm skipping this as I've already shown the example in the story)
(use 1-3 main points per body)			

Conclusion	Talker	Middleman	Scriptwriter
List the main points you've talked about.	re	how to free up day	So what I presented here is a technique that helps you free your day in order to work on the really important stuff.
Activity / application / practical exercise in which they can put the information into practice.	apply example	move tasks last Thursday as far away as possible add imp. project	Now it's time to test it out. Take your list of tasks and move them to the last Thursday of the month. Move every task as far away as possible, leaving only the really urgent ones on your list. Then, add your most important project to it and start working!
Teaser for the following content. The "what comes next" part.	The one and only despi-cable Thursday	The despicable Thursday => next video	But what happens with on that cold, cold Thursday? The one where all your tasks migrated to? Find out how you can manage that day efficiently and without a headache in the next lesson!

Now it's your turn!
Fill the table below and show me your work!

Introduction	Talker	Middleman	Scriptwriter
Why should they listen?			
What are you going to talk about?			
In which situation can they put the information into practice?			

Body	Talker	Middleman	Scriptwriter
Story that illustrates main point, agitates the problem and may or may not deliver the solution			
Main point			
Example of applying main point			
(use 1-3 main points per body)			

Conclusion	Talker	Middleman	Scriptwriter
List the main points you've talked about.			
Activity / application / practical exercise in which they can put the information into practice.			
Teaser for the following content. The "what comes next" part.			

The Meta Project

My motto is: "I teach students how to become their own teachers!" And the goal of the meta project is exactly that. To show your students how to achieve what they want using the methods presented in your course.

A meta project's main objective is to deliver tangible results to your students. Its other objectives are to create engagement, get testimonials and case studies, and show to the students that the course is real and that it delivers on its promises.

Lesson projects, exercises, quizzes and practice activities help students practice a concept that they've learned. And the meta project gathers everything together into something that's big and inspiring. Here, your students have the chance to put in the real world what they learn in the videos.

That's exactly why courses like Ruby on Rails in 30 Days (http://bit.ly/roby30) and Expert Screenflow Skills (http://courses.vaidabogdan.com) are so successful. The former helps the students build an application in 30 days and the latter has 4 applicable video editing projects.

Your meta project:
- If there were one thing that the student would be able to do after finishing your course which would be it? (E.g. For video editing: the ability to masterfully edit a video of himself teaching in front of the camera. For time management: to have a system that takes care of all her tasks and that shows her only the next step that needs to get done.)
- Say why the project is important, how it will help them and that you will be there to help them every step of the way. Connect the meta project with the course outcomes.
- Ask your students why they joined and what they will do with the things they are about to learn. In what context will they apply them? Can you replicate that context? (E.g. If it's a course on writing professional resumes, the first X buyers of the course will have their resumes reviewed by 3 top HR consultants.)
- Use quora.com to get ideas for projects in your field. Here's my profile (https://www.quora.com/profile/Bogdan-Vaida/) and my response to "What are the new methods for teaching that engage students in the learning process?" (http://bit.ly/quora-methods) and "For physical security courses which training formats exist, other than slides?" (http://bit.ly/quora-training)
- Just ASK (http://amzn.to/1LrtsVb)! Ask your students what they like to do as a course project. Offer your whole support and see what they come up with. Then, create a public poll and ask them to vote.
- Ask me for ideas.

- Launch your course *without* the meta project. (I know: Sacrilege!) And then ask the buyers, because it's in their direct interest.

My meta project called _____ **will helps the student build/create/finance/program/launch/release** _____ **in** __ **days.**

Chapter 3: Convert visitors into loyal customers with a great course presentation

Purpose: Most instructors think that delivering great content is 80% of the work and the rest is sales & marketing. Sales people, on the other hand, know that nobody will buy a course if they don't know it exists. Great content sells by itself *after* it gets a critical mass of students. In this video I'll be helping you craft a presentation for your course that will convert visitors into loyal students.

Mandatory steps: (2 hours)
1. The easiest way to create a course presentation is to follow a ready-made template like The Course Presentation Template.

2.   Just in case you need to create an image for the course, make it:
a.   Relevant.
b.   Mobile friendly.
c.   Simple, with clear text (the course title or a powerful quote).
d.   With a good contrast between the icon/picture and the background.
e.   Focused on one thing.
f.   Professional. Get a designer for the course image either on Fiverr.com or on Upwork.com. And if you are publishing on Udemy, they can create the image for you (https://info.udemy.com/course-image-design-gift.html).

The biggest mistake most people make at this point is delaying the writing process. Yes, it needs to sell but why not create it first and optimize the text after, maybe with the help of one of the communities I listed in the optional steps. It's way better to quickly create something you can work with rather than indefinitely postpone a masterpiece.

Optional steps:
- Make some of your lectures available without paying (free preview) so your future students will know what they get.
- Read copywriting articles on Copyblogger (http://www.copyblogger.com/) or join the forum at American Writers & Artists Inc (http://www.awaionline.com/).
- Join one of these paid membership sites where you can get feedback on your copy (and much more):
  o   Next Level Group Mastermind (Ryan Levesque) - $97/mo (http://www.nextlevelgroupmastermind.com/)

- Copy Chief (Kevin Rogers) - $97/mo (http://copychief.com/join/)

- Digital Marketer (Ryan Deiss) - $37/mo (http://www.digitalmarketer.com/)

The Course Presentation Template

Test Your Personality Using The DISC Assessment Tool

Persuade, motivate and inspire others by understanding their personality!

🛒 Enroll in Course for $97

Why should you become a student?

- to **directly apply a world renowned test and identify your personality** (Fortune 500 companies use DISC to screen their employees for specific hiring traits)
- to access a practical tool that has real world applications in:
  - **influencing and motivating others**
  - **winning friends**
  - **improving relationships** (you will understand your spouse's secret language especially when she looks strange at you and says the ubiquitous "nothing" or when he is hyper aggressive with his own quality time)

You have 3 ways of doing this: shortest form, short form and long form.

Short form works great as a script for your video presentation while long form works better for your text presentation. I'm saying this (well, writing actually) because it's pretty difficult to maintain the attention of a student in very long videos.

My recommendation is to start with writing the shortest presentation needed to launch the course and then improve as needed.

The quickest, shortest form:
1. Write a catchphrase or ask them a question to hook their interest.
2. Add bullet points with important benefits.
3. Write a summary of the content, list what the course covers and show the benefits of each section.
4. Give them a one liner consisting of what they will gain or how is it useful for them.

5. Tell them how it is taught (exercises, demonstrating on video, self-paced).
6. Underline what tangible outcomes they will achieve by the end of the course.
7. Add a call to action restating why they should join.

The short form:
1. Welcome the readers and introduce yourself. (Use talking-head footage.)
2. Show the benefits of the course in terms of what the students are getting after completing it.
   a. Don't talk about what they'll be learning. (Remember the questions you asked when you were little: "Why should I learn history?" Would you have been satisfied with the answer: "To learn about the war"?)
   b. Instead, talk about what they will be able to do after learning occurs. ("History repeats itself. With a thorough understanding of history, you will be able to predict things to come.")
   c. Speak in images. Don't say "you will know a lot of Photoshop tricks like background removal". Instead, say "you will be able to replace the background in any image so as to move the actor into a spectacular scene, near a waterfall, for example."
3. Next, list the topics that you'll be covering in your course.
   a. For each topic, show the benefits -- what will they be getting?
   b. Make sure to phrase the lesson name in a very captivating way; don't teach "How to use the Spot Healing Brush" when you can say "Repair small areas of an image using the Spot Healing Brush".

4. Tell them whom this course is for.
    a.   "This course is for advanced programmers ready to dive into the ins and outs of how the operating system works."
    b.   Show you understand them by talking about their challenges or their goals: "If you want to be a great team player but you have trouble with some of your teammates, this course will give you 3 ways to connect with them at a deep level, to inspire them .."
5. Make a call to action.
    a.   Tell them to join <u>now</u>.
    b.   Ideally, give a reason why they should join now and not later.
        i.   The first X students get 1 hour of free coaching from you.
        ii.   The price may increase in the future.
        iii.   Course will be closed after the group is formed.
        iv.   You will use the feedback of the first X people to provide additional materials specific to their needs.
        v.   Becoming a founding member also gives them access to X, Y and Z.
    c.   You can also explain the process, what will happen after they click the button, what to expect inside (tempting them to join).

That's it. And you can use this form for both video and written text. But then, you would probably ask yourself- what's the difference? Should you do both or should you do one over the other?

Here's my answer:
    • Text is great when quoting numbers or dates that change. For example the last date this course was uploaded, the number of students inside the course, the number of

reviews, some updates that you've made (e.g. you added videos for a new feature of the software).

• Video is perfect for inspiration and immersion. You can show the viewers a sequence of you editing a video (for a video editing course), or a short animation from inside the course. This whets their appetite for the rest of the content.

• Text can be skimmed. Maybe they want to see testimonials or the curriculum and they hate persuasion through emotional stories.

I would recommend doing both if your platform allows. The viewer can always stop the video or ignore the text.

Now, I'm making a call to action: "Go and shoot your promo video!"

The longest form:

This is the most difficult way to write. My recommendation for writing a long sales letter is the 12-Step Foolproof Sales Letter Template (http://www.marketingprofs.com/2/frey2.asp) or hiring a professional copywriter.

BONUS (requested by the readers) — General guidelines:

- Create an alluring headline, subhead line and opening paragraph. They are the first things the prospect sees when he/she opens the page. (Check "The 4 U's Approach" for information on how to do that.)
- Writing style:
  - Speak in the second person.
  - Talk to 8th graders. Describe the process, what they will get and never assume they know what you know.
  - Use familiarity, show genuine interest and talk using their language. E.g. For programmers, replace: "Hello" with "Hello world". Why? It's an inside joke only programmers know :)
- Show the benefits:
  - Sell by talking about their pain, but promise pleasure to keep them reading.
  - List the table of contents, show how each video links to their problem and helps them overcome it.
  - When creating lists of 3-5 benefits, make the last one an out-of-this-universe benefit. E.g. "This time management technique also helped me get over my divorce". It helps both in connecting with the audience and in maintaining attention.
- When talking about yourself you can use a shorter version of The Hero's Journey (http://bit.ly/herojourney1). Here's another version: http://bit.ly/herojourney2 .
- When showing credentials, instead of flaunting them, display logos of companies you worked with or other visible tokens of authority. Don't write, show!
- Validate potential results they may get with success stories, testimonials from previous students, statistics or (other) real word examples.

- Highlight the testimonials that are specific (I've underlined the words that show specificity in the examples below).
- Product testimonials:
    - How did it improve their life? "Product is helpful." vs. "With the help of technique X from the second video I was able to create a Star Wars effect for my upcoming movie!"
    - From worst to best: "20 days after finishing the exercises mentioned at the end of the course I was able to do 100 pushups. Thank you Bogdan!"
- Character testimonials:
    - You stuck with them until they got results.
    - You went over the top to make sure they got it.
- If you don't have testimonials you can get them using the following technique (if the Terms of Service of your course marketplace allows it):
    - Message students that arrived at 90% of the content and ask them for feedback. An action valuable in itself.
    - Ask the enthusiastic responders for a real life situation where they applied the techniques.
    - Upon receiving the story, ask them if they would be willing to share this information when they review the course.
- While reading the course presentation or while listening to the video, the prospect will ask himself the following questions, make sure you answer them:
    - Attention needed: (when viewing the course page) What am I doing here?

- Trust needed: Does she know my situation? Did it happen to her too?
      - Solution needed: It hurts, what now? Can you help? Is this right for me?
      - Credentials needed: Who is she? Why should I trust her? Do I like her?
      - Benefits needed: How does this help me?
      - Testimonials needed: Does it work? Did the product help others like me?
- Add bonuses:
   - They need to complement your course content.
   - But your students shouldn't need them in order to finish the course.
   - Bonuses exist to make the work easier/faster/cheaper.
   - Examples:
      - Demos, source code, additional exercises.
      - Motivating success stories.
      - Worksheets or templates.
      - Deals and discounted products that may reduce production costs or decrease delivery time.
- My complete list of courses can be found at http://courses.vaidabogdan.com . Get some inspiration!

DAY 3: PRODUCE CONTENT THAT TRANSFORMS!

Chapter 1: Set up a cheap but effective recording studio

Purpose: Delivering high quality videos with awesome audio is not that expensive. If you follow some simple tips you can get all the necessary equipment for under $200. Even cheaper if you own a smartphone with a good camera (and who doesn't, nowadays!).

Mandatory steps: (1 hour)
1. Read the Technical Equipment section for recommendations on what to buy and what not to buy. (Hint: You only need an iPhone for the minimum. And you can go even more frugal than that by screencasting!)
2. Check the Recording Guidelines section to setup your software equipment.
3. Test your setup. You have no idea how many times I forgot something, from pushing record on my microphone to having the sunlight smile on half of my face.

a.   Record a one minute video explaining how to tie your shoes (http://bit.ly/tieshoes1). Or, if you prefer, teach a mini-bonus for your course.
b.   Send it to friends or post it on Facebook and ask for feedback.
c.   If the marketplace where you are posting your online course has a forum or social group, post it there too.
d.   Ideally, also give the video to your potential audience.
e.   Listen to the feedback and fix whatever bugs.

The biggest mistake most people make at this point is investing too much in their equipment. Why invest now when you can invest from the money you earn when your course goes live? Buy the minimum necessary equipment to launch your course and upgrade after.

Optional steps:
- From A to Z: creating a talking head video (http://bit.ly/talkinghead1) — includes lighting setup, writing the script, etc.
- In this chapter, YouTube is god of all information. Use it:
  - To check reviews for equipment you can get a discount for.
  - To see how a specific camera records and hear how a specific mic records.
  - For DIY projects (like your own microphone pop filter or prompter).
  - To set up a very cheap studio.
  - To improve your voice or body language.
- Also read How To DIY: Home Studio Setup for Video Production (http://bit.ly/diy-studio).

Technical Equipment

If you want to go cheap, record your screen and voice while you show a PowerPoint/Keynote/ Prezi presentation. No need for any investment.

If you don't want to film yourself, go and buy a good microphone. Laptop microphones aren't good enough and audio is more important than video.

And if you want to go all in, here are the priorities:
1. A smartphone with a good camera, a good lavaliere mic connected to it and a tripod.
2. 2 lights for your studio.
3. A white backdrop.
4. 2 more lights.
5. A better camera.
6. A professional setup.

Video equipment

In case you want to actually appear on video, here are some great cameras you can buy:

1. Use your (i)phone camera. iPhone 5 (http://amzn.to/1SZOgLq) is good enough and iPhone 6s (http://amzn.to/1SZOjXQ) has a great camera that can compete with some DSLRs (just make sure you take the 64GB version because you really need that space; the videos are HUGE). Here's how the video looks: https://youtu.be/s3u_FRz-4RA .

2. Webcams like Logitech C920 (http://amzn.to/1SZOnqB). C920 is a good enough camera that I've used for my first few courses (https://youtu.be/3e843kgT4nQ).

3. Or any other camera as long as it records 720p and it has good reviews.

4. You also need a tripod (http://amzn.to/1Vxv2KW) and a camera mount (that you can usually buy with the camera).

Audio equipment

1. When screencasting, narrating slides or speaking in front of the camera I definitely recommend Blue Microphones Yeti USB Microphone (http://amzn.to/1SZP4jy). Here's how it sounds: https://youtu.be/A1Ij8VsR4eo . The cheaper alternative is Blue Microphones Snowball USB Microphone (http://amzn.to/1mQHrNL) which lacks most controls and fine-tuning but is good enough and at half the price. The Snowball doesn't have an option to reduce the background noise (which the Yeti has) but it can still be done with the help of software. Same for Samson Go Mic (http://amzn.to/1mQIRIa); cheaper, and good enough.
2. When you deliver a talking head video, I recommend a lavaliere mic like ATR 3350 (http://amzn.to/1SZQ3jV) or Sony ECMCS3 (http://amzn.to/1SZQ7Qp). If you want to make only one investment in audio, take the Blue Yeti and put it just outside of the video frame and the audio will still be good).
3. Connect your lavaliere mic with:

a.   Your video camera so that you record in sync. If you are recording via your smartphone you can use an adapter like this one (http://www.kvconnection.com/product-p/km-iphone-mic.htm), for the iPhone, to record the audio through your phone.

b.   Your computer (if you are using a webcam).

c.   A voice recorder like Sony ICD PX333 (http://amzn.to/1mQK0zy) or Sony ICD-UX71 (http://amzn.to/1mQJWjg). Here's how my voice sounds when using ATR 3350 and Sony ICD-UX71: https://youtu.be/pQUc-c6gvos?t=23s .

Software

If you're using a Mac, Screenflow (http://bit.ly/screenflowfeatures) is one of the best screencasting and video editing applications on the market. It's extremely easy to use, it has a very intuitive interface, it lets you edit your videos, add images/text/music/transitions and it comes with a lot of other cool stuff. If you are interested in mesmerizing your audience with the help of Screenflow, check my project-based course (http://bit.ly/screenflow-3doc) on doing exactly that. As a bonus, you'll also see how I applied this template to create the course. (The link has a special offer for the buyers of this course.)

A Windows alternative to Screenflow is Camtasia (http://www.techsmith.com). It's Screenflow's twin sister.

A free solution for both Windows and Mac is Jing (https://www.techsmith.com/jing.html). It doesn't let you do any video editing but it records your screen and microphone.

For slides, we have Keynote (http://www.apple.com/mac/keynote/), PowerPoint (http://office.microsoft.com/en-us/powerpoint/) and Prezi (http://www.prezi.com).

And if you will be delivering via talking head, you will benefit from buying a prompter app for your tablet. For iOS, I recommend Voice Prompt (http://www.voicepromptapp.com/ — which has a great feature: the text follows your voice) or Teleprompt+ (http://www.bombingbrain.com/teleprompt.html — where you need to manually adjust the speed of the text). For Android, there is Simple Teleprompter (http://bit.ly/simple-teleprompter).

David Malki shows you how to create your own teleprompter, for free. Check his YouTube video here: https://youtu.be/xxIE-xBzbeA .

Also check out the Free Multimedia Guide (http://freemultimediaguide.vaidabogdan.com/) to access thousands of royalty free images, music and videos.

Other equipment
If using the "talking head":
   1. Lighting:
a.   After audio quality, lighting is key to recording great videos. You can go free using natural light: just film yourself outdoors, during the day, when the sun is up.
b.   Or, you can **D**o **I**t **Y**ourself: DIY Office Video Studio (http://wistia.com/library/diy-office-video-studio) or Down and Dirty Lighting Kit (http://wistia.com/library/down-and-dirty-lighting-kit).
c.   You can even invest in VL-9026S (http://amzn.to/1SZRij3).
d.   A minimum for indoor is a 2-point lighting setup: http://bit.ly/2-point .
e.   The main idea is to keep it bright and to have minimal shadows.
   2. Backdrop:
a.   A blank wall or a minimal background if you want to go for the free version. And, if possible, unfocus the background using the camera.
b.   White (http://amzn.to/1mQLTMy) or black (http://amzn.to/1SZRS03) background. (Make sure to check the sizes).
c.   Create a contrast between your clothes with the background, you need to stand out.

If hearing strong "P"s, "B"s or air pressure, consider buying a pop filter (http://amzn.to/1UgqWbw) for your microphone. You can also make one (https://youtu.be/WcB3s8KOk4w).

If using your cellphone to record, you can buy:

1. A cell phone tripod adapter like the iPhone Tripod Mount (http://amzn.to/1RZt6rf).
2. A bluetooth camera shutter remote control (http://amzn.to/22rsy8g).

The image you see here was done using my "good enough" equipment- the trusted 2-point lighting set up. Not *that* bad... right?

Recording Guidelines

Save As:	3DOC-Success-Story-5.mp4

Where: 🖿 Desktop

Preset: Web - High

H.264 video encoding at 1 200 kbits/sec. AAC audio encoding at 256 kbits/sec.

Customize...   Manage...

Dimensions: ⦿ Scale by 100 ⌄ to 1920 x 1080

○ Scale to custom size

Options: ☐ Use Motion Blur

☐ Add Chapter Track from Markers

☐ Add Captions Track

?   Cancel   Export

Background sounds:
- Close outside windows to prevent noise (police cars, shouts).
- Check for other noise sources (vents, fans and electronic devices).
- Put your phone (and computer) on silent.

Camera positioning:
- Use a tripod.
- Place it at eye level.

Lighting setup:
- Two Point Lighting – How To Set Up Basic Online Video Lighting (http://bit.ly/2-point-b).
- Complete Guide to Three-Point Lighting (http://bit.ly/3-point).

Video recording settings:
(depends on the platform where you're going to publish, but here are some good pointers)

- HD: 720p
- Compression: H.264
- Aspect ratio: 16:9
- Resolution: 1280x720
- Frame rate: 10-15
- Frame reordering: uncheck
- Key frames: Automatic
- Data rate: Automatic

Video export settings:
These are generic recommendations. The platform where you upload your course will probably have some very specific criteria for the export settings.

- Video compression: H.264 or MPEG-4
- Data rate/bit rate: 3000 kbps/seconds
- Aspect ratio: 16:9
- Dimensions: 1280x720
- Frame rate: 30 fps

Chapter 2: 3, 2, 1, Action!

Purpose: To maximize your students' learning potential you need to have a strong delivery. Delivering in front of the camera or via a microphone may seem burdensome at first, but with practice, it's a very useful skill to develop. In this chapter you will learn some very helpful techniques to deliver your content.

Mandatory steps: (6 hours)
1. Learn how to be your best and Deliver Great Content! This is your quick recap on best practices for delivering content :)
2. 3, 2, 1, Action! Record all your content at once.

a.   We're doing all the writing at once, all the recording at once and all the editing at once, so you don't have to switch tasks and tools, deploy a studio or change your frame of mind. You only need to do one thing at a time.

b.   The course presentation video can be a talking head or a slides narration of your written text. You can even leave it in text form if your course platform allows it.

3.   Enthrall your audience using The Dazzling Effect!
4.   Remember the chapter where you contacted your followers in order to get feedback on your written copy? Do the same for the people that responded to your previous request and frame it as giving them access to future paid content.

The biggest mistake most people make at this point is concentrating on video rather than audio. They expect to speak about the topic and for the audience to just listen. But it doesn't work that way! Maintaining the audience's attention with highly engaging (and, if possible, interactive) content while transfer of learning occurs is quite tricky and my best advice here is to concentrate on your voice and audio delivery. If the audio is great, the video can be forgiven. However, nobody will forgive a bad audio.

Optional steps:
1. If you need more information, examples or tips & tricks on a particular topic, ask me and I'll make sure to 1. answer your questions and 2. update this guide with the new material.
2. Do a course like Expert Screenflow Skills (http://bit.ly/screenflow-3doc) or Video Genesis (http://bit.ly/video-genesis-3doc) to improve your video editing skills.
3. Read the short article 6 Tips to Make Video Editing Easier (http://bit.ly/video-editing-3doc).

Deliver Great Content

In this section I'm going to provide you with some of the best tips I'm using to deliver enthralling composition. If you want to go deeper on a particular topic, just ask and I'll be happy to oblige.

General tips:
- Rehearse the transcript once or twice before filming. It helps as you'll know where the pauses should be and where you should use more (or less) body language.
- Get in the mood: listen to playful music or do some crazy dancing around.
- Get Loose for the Camera (http://bit.ly/get-loose-3doc).
- Read Resonate: Present Visual Stories that Transform Audiences by Nancy Duarte (http://amzn.to/1qXe8Kh) and slide:ology: The Art and Science of Creating Great Presentations (http://amzn.to/1oWMjmf).

Voice tips:
- Audio is more important than video. (Proof: Watch a thriller on mute vs. a movie without video. Which one do you understand better?) Focus on how you sound, not on how you look.
- Speak clearly! Not all of your listeners will be native English speakers.
- Demonstrate excitement and enthusiasm for the topic.
- Place smooth surface under the microphone to tune out sound reflections from the desk.
- Move your computer away from the microphone so you won't record the fans.

Optimize for later editing:
- Always do a first take to check your setup:
  - Video records properly. Camera settings are correct.
  - You are focused and in the center of the video.
  - Lighting is good.
  - Audio is clear. (You have no idea how many times my voice recorder battery went dead and I didn't realize until after the first video.)
  - No other noises are heard.
  - I'm part of a Facebook mastermind group where instructors ask for feedback on their courses before the launch. It helped me tremendously. Wherever you're going to deliver your course, they probably have a similar service. Join in and ask for feedback!
- When you start recording, don't speak for the first 5 seconds. You'll use the dead space later, to filter the background noise.
- When you make a mistake don't repeat the last word; after cutting, it sounds distorted. Instead, repeat the whole sentence. This way, you can cut the bad sentence and leave the improved one.

- Also, when you make a mistake and you need to remove the previous part, clap your hands 3 times. What this does is create a loud noise that you can identify on the audio track which makes it easy to jump to that section and remove the bad sentence.
- Never edit while recording. Do a recording day and an editing day. It's easier to get in that particular frame of mind.
- Don't delete the takes where you had a lot of mistakes! You can mix them up in a funny video or a blooper (https://youtu.be/3l-r5yjmNeI?t=160) at the end of your instructional video. It shows off your personality.

Talking head:
- I recommend you set the framing (http://www.mediacollege.com/video/shots/) to MCU (Medium Close Up) as in the first picture or MS (Mid Shot) as in the second.

- Smile on camera and exaggerate your enthusiasm (as the energy is usually lost on video, especially when talking to a wall).
- Use direct eye contact. Look directly at the audience. Quick tip: put a small figurine on your camera or a picture of your best friend and talk to it.
- And, as an additional resource, read: 11 Pro Tips for Unmissable Talking Head Videos: http://bit.ly/talking-head-3doc .

Prompter tips:
- Position the camera at least 9 ft. from where you'll deliver, at eye level, and the prompter just above it. Never position the camera less than 6 ft. from you because your audience will notice how your eyes are reading the text from the prompter.
- Don't switch between looking at the camera and at the prompter. If you keep looking at the prompter, on video you will appear as if looking directly at the audience.

Presentations:
- Never add more than 3 bullets/points/ideas per slide.

Make your choice!

A. write graduation paper

B. write the introduction to the graduation paper

You can access the rest of the materials here:
http://time.onlinepersonalitytests.org

- Show an image that is representative to the content (ideally a big image).

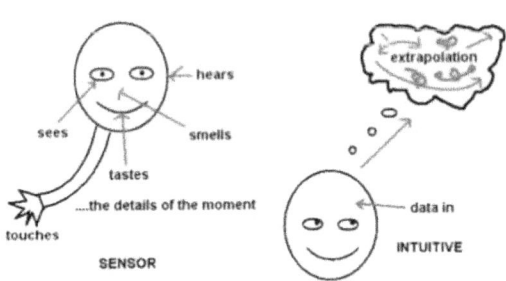

Narrating presentations:
- The process is simple:
  - You start your screen recording.
  - Then you start playing the slides.
  - And while the slides play, you narrate the content that you want to deliver.
- A trick to perfectly match the audio with the slides is:
  - Record your audio by expressively reading from your script. Ignore slides at this point.
  - Start the screen recording application, play the audio and move your slides in sync with the audio. At this point you are not recording your voice, you are only move the slides.
  - When editing, use the original audio and the slides recording. You will instantly "marry" the 2, without needing to mix and match the timings.

The Dazzling Effect

General recommendations:
- Most steps are optional. You only need to cut the beginning (before you start speaking), the end (after you've stopped speaking) and any other sentences you may have repeated due to mistakes.
- Collect all of your mistakes and create a short, 5-second blooper at the end of the video. You can also add them at the end of the promo video — they show personality.
- After editing, play the whole video one more time to verify your work.
- Don't forget: never edit while recording. Do a recording session followed by an editing session.
- Complement your videos with royalty free music, images and video footage. Here's one of the best directories (http://freemultimediaguide.vaidabogdan.com/) of royalty free sites.

Look like you know your stuff:
A person speaking in front of the camera gets boring after 5'
(and even sooner). Use visual tools to reinforce what you're
telling your audience.

- Make it mobile friendly: use big text. Bigger than big
  actually, so it can be seen on an iPhone screen.
- As I've explained in the *Deliver Great Content* chapter,
  you should set the framing
  (http://www.mediacollege.com/video/shots/) to MCU
  or MS. If you forgot to do this, you can still fix it in the
  editor.
- Play with the color controls, especially if your
  background is not homogenous or if you don't have
  enough lights. Increase the brightness level by 20-50%
  and you'll appear to have a professional studio.
  Saturation can also help. For Screenflow video editing
  course, I chose the following settings:

  ▼ Color Controls

Saturation:		128%
Brightness:		155%
Contrast:		108%

- And, of course, really know your stuff!

Sound like a professional:
- Edit out all uhms, (long) pauses and mistakes
  (grammatical and pronunciation-wise). You can leave
  small mistakes in, especially if you were doing a
  "talking head" so as not to have too many cuts.
- A lot of sound editing programs have the option to
  identify background noise and cut it. If yours has it, do
  it. Screenflow has that option in the Audio tab ->
  Remove Background Noise. Other programs need to

analyze a "silent" section of your audio to filter that noise.

- Check for your claps on the audio track, the ones you made after making a mistake, and quickly remove the problematic sentence (found before the clap).

Expertly edit the narrated presentations:
- Move the audio 0.5 seconds before the video so that you start speaking when the slide appears, not a few milliseconds after.
- Since you are not appearing in the video, speed it by 10%. This will create a more dynamic experience for the listeners.

Special effects for the presentation video:
- Use footage from your activities (in order to create trust, fun and immersion):
    - Footage related to the topic. E.g. You can show authority by showing footage of you, presenting the topic at a conference.
    - Unrelated footage. E.g. You snowboard, jump, stop in front of the camera and then say: "The following video contains scenes that some viewers may find enlightening!" Revealing parts of your private life can be used to show personality, creativity and to develop trust.

- o Here's some inspiration: https://www.masterclass.com/classes/usher-teaches-the-art-of-performance .
- Show results other participants got. E.g. Videos from their lives, what they achieved with your help, the car they bought after doubling their income due to your programming course, etc.
- For fun: show bloopers or behind the scenes footage.

Chapter 3: Publish your magnum opus!

Purpose: Do you really need a purpose here? :) Just follow the steps and hit that publish button!

Mandatory steps: (1 hour)
1. Add bonus materials that make their work faster, cheaper, better or easier:

a. The bonuses should *complement* the product. Don't consider bonuses, materials that should have been in the product from the start.

b. An example of a bonus for a course on how to create an online course is a huge discount to a video editing course. That's why I'm giving you this link (http://bit.ly/screenflow-3doc) where you can get my Expert Screenflow Skills course for 50% off. (You see what you get just by being attentive?)

c. Bonuses sweeten the deal. Undecided prospects suddenly buy after finding out that a particular bonus helps them save even more money.

2. Find the right price using The Perfect Price Challenge.

The biggest mistake most people make at this point is thinking too much (again!). Set a price, launch your course. That's it, no more thinking. For your first course, thinking should be done when reality shouts: "the price is too high", not beforehand.

Optional steps:
- Create coupons with special offers. Never advertise your coupons, just give them when needed.
- When a new course is born, access is given to a few family members with the explicit condition of taking care of it. Give 5-10 people free access to your course in order to receive valuable feedback. They will scrutinize the adorable entity and provide you with relevant suggestions.

The Perfect Price Challenge

I won't bore you with classical advice stolen from the internet like "You always underestimate how much your course is worth", yada yada. I'm also not going to talk about membership sites, continuity and other such things. The whole program assists you in creating a course during the weekend, not in building a flagship product polished and edited to perfection.

So I'm going to give you 2 other routes you can go: the fastest route and the best route.
And, of course, it's completely up to you to make the choice.

The fastest route

1. Launch your course for free to get an initial audience and feedback for your content.
   or
2. Set the price to roughly $20-$50/hour of course content (since it's your first product).

Also, the price depends on the topic you choose to teach. Business, IT and finance courses are more expensive while personal development, lifestyle and language courses are less expensive. But don't worry about this on your first course, just set the price using the recommendations above and launch it.

The best route: The Perfect Price Challenge

I've successfully used this technique to launch 2 of my courses (and to sell some offline trainings). The second course I used this technique on, I had 219 total customers and got 412 email responses.

So, what's it all about? Easy, just send 2 emails to your followers:

In the first one, tell them about the course you will be offering, the benefits they will be getting and show them the course curriculum. Then, give them 5 prices and ask them to choose what they think the course price will be. And promise to give one of the winners free access to the course.

Basically, they write "a)" or "e)"... and they get a chance to join your course for free.
After the challenge ends, check the statistics and choose the price a level below the choice with the most responses.
E.g. If most people chose $130 as the course price, and the lower tier is $97 then set your course price to $97.
What you are basically doing is making them an offer. The course price is a bit lower than what they expected so they get *a better deal.*
If you don't have a mailing list, just ask your audience manually and then make them an offer of 15% below that mark.

Here's my email asking people to guess the price of my course:

"

(if you're interested in the contest, read the whole mail)

Hi,
Today I want to tell you about a revelation I had, while reading

<u>Contagious, Why Things Catch On</u>, a revelation about
the psychology of sales.

If we see something that's on sale, especially if there's a great
discount, we suppose we're lucky enough to be able to take
advantage of it. On the other hand, if the price is the normal one,
we don't think of it as a great opportunity.

In the book, Jonah Berger speaks of the Rule of 100.

Imagine you're looking at a 20$ t-shirt and that you have to
choose between:

a) a 25% discount
b) a 5$ discount

Which one sounds better?

Comparing results in shop sales, Jonah noticed a clear difference
between the 2 options. People prefer the first one, <u>the 25% discount</u>.

But what happens if we increase the price?

Now you have to choose a MacBook laptop valued at 2000$, which:

a) has a 25% discount
b) has a 500$ discount.

Which discount sounds better?
Yes, you've guessed it! It's b), <u>the 500$ discount</u>.

The same discount seems greater when presented in percentages for
sums lower than 100$, and it seems greater when presented as a
figure, when the sums are greater than 100$.

I personally tested the Rule of 100 (+ CONTEST)

Last spring I released a time management course that I offered

for 200$. After the success that the course had, I sent a mail
to my first series of students, offering a 25% discount for the next course
that I was preparing for the members of the Online Personality Tests
community (the only condition was to give me continuous feedback
as they go through the modules).

I didn't mention the price in the e-mail, I only wanted to know
how many of them were interested before knowing the price
and how many would still be interested after knowing it.

I've received emails from some participants asking me
if it would be more than 400$, but when they found out the final price,
they were relieved. The same discount, but as a fixed amount,
I sent to the second series of students.

The result? More people from the first series invested in the training.

Now I would like to propose a contest that you can participate in,
to win access to the new online course that I told you about.

What the course contains (per chapters):
1) Identify your personality type once and for all
2) Understand the personality of others (+4 practical exercises)
3) Causes of stress and solutions for each
4) How to change our personality type (+4 practical exercises)
5) Communication channels between personality types
6) Your personal development plan
7) Other resources (deepen your studies)

I won't give you more details because I want this contest to have
an element of luck. So tell me: What do you think the price for the
course is (without discount)?

a) 597$
b) 397$
c) 297$
d) 197$
e) 97$

Your future strategy

Once you get some sales going, you can test different prices in
order to get a better return on investment (ROI). In the image
attached, I set the price to $25 and got 20 sales, $50 and got 8
sales and the next test provided a very nice sweet spot of 15
sales at $40.

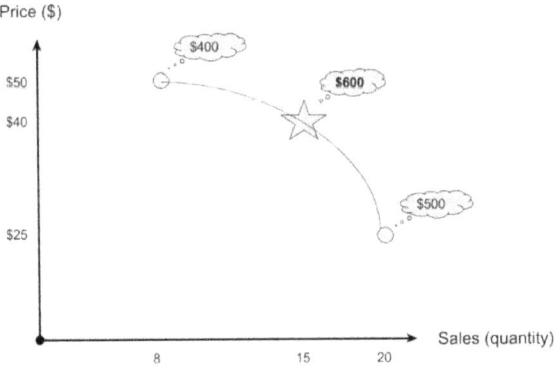

When testing the price also think of:
- Word of mouth marketing. Maybe by setting the price lower and letting more students in, you will get a lot of reviews, great testimonials and word of mouth marketing.
- Payment plans and monthly payments.
- Leveraging bonuses and improving the course presentation to create a better offer.

Also, you can invite your students to fill in a survey where you ask them how they perceived the course price in relation to the received content.

And remember: people don't buy the content, they buy the package (the course presentation), after which they receive the content. So the course price never reflects your content's value, it reflects how you've packaged it, the perceived value. Your content's value is reflected by reviews, testimonials, refunds and long term customers.

Finally, here is a good article on setting the right price for online content: http://www.tagoras.com/pricing-online-learning/ .

My course price is: …………………………………..

WHAT'S NEXT?

BONUS: Access the video course that this book was based upon

This book started out as a workbook for the video course that I launched on http://www.courseology.org .
If you want to get the video version of the methods described in the book, together with visual examples, case studies, bonus materials (like "The 5 toxic mentalities that sabotage your success"), lessons on video equipment and much more, forward me (office@vaidabogdan.com) the proof of payment that you've received when you purchased this book to receive an even better deal for the online course.

Final words - your next steps to ensure a successful launch

That's it, my friend! Over the past 3 days you've worked tirelessly to build this masterpiece. And now that you've published it, take one hour to play a game of Heroes of the Storm, Hearthstone or Starcraft 2 (http://www.blizzard.com). I'm on the EU servers with nickname Zeratul#23300 .

Really! Relax, and enjoy the moment.

And after you're done relaxing, tell me what one thing I should add to this course that will make it at least 20% better. I was thinking of a bonus day, day 4, dedicated to marketing. What do you say?

Don't forget that I am here for you in case of any problems you may encounter in your endeavor. Contact me (at office@vaidabogdan.com) with any questions you may have. I promise to answer, and to also update the content based on your needs. You can find my contact info on my website: www.vaidabogdan.com .
And if you are interested in learning more about teaching online, course creation, education, trainer training and other similar subjects, join my mailing list by entering your email on the same page.

Finished your course? Send me a link! I'd love to give you some feedback and help you improve it.

www.ingramcontent.com/pod-product-compliance
Lightning Source LLC
Chambersburg PA
CBHW060356190526
45169CB00002B/616